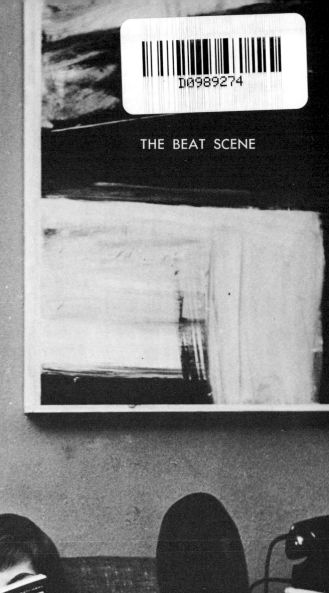

THE BEAT SCENE

Jack Kerouac reading at the Artist's Studio

# The Beat Scene

PHOTOGRAPHS BY *Fred McDarrah*

EDITED AND

WITH AN INTRODUCTION BY *Elias Wilentz*

*Corinth Books,* NEW YORK, 1960

DISTRIBUTED BY *The Citadel Press*

Second Printing, April 1961

Corinth Books are published by Corinth Books, Inc.
32 West Eighth Street, New York 11, New York.

This Corinth Book is distributed by The Citadel Press, Inc.
222 Fourth Avenue, New York 3, New York.

# Acknowledgments

The editor wishes to express his thanks to the persons and publishers listed below for their kind cooperation in granting permission to reprint material.

*Tentative Description of a Dinner Given to Promote the Impeachment of President Eisenhower,* by Lawrence Ferlinghetti. Copyright 1958 by Lawrence Ferlinghetti. Published by Golden Mountain Press as a booklet distributed by City Lights, 261 Columbus Avenue, San Francisco 11, California.

*Making It!* by Seymour Krim. An abridged version appeared in The Village Voice. Copyright 1959 by The Village Voice.

Extensive quotation in the Introduction from a statement by Allen Ginsberg, Gregory Corso and Peter Orlovsky. The statement appeared as a letter in the Spring 1959 issue of the Wagner Literary Magazine. Quotation is made with the kind permission of the Authors and of the faculty advisor, Willard Maas.

*The Gift* by Robert Creeley. Copyright 1960 by Folio Magazine, Spring 1960 issue.

*Over a Beer* by Jonathan Williams. Copyright 1959 by Jonathan Williams and Fielding Dawson. From *Empire Finals at Verona* by the Authors, Jargon Book.

*The Apology* by David Galler. Copyright 1960 by Carleton Miscellany, Spring 1960 issue.

To other literary magazines and publications in which some of the writings may have appeared. This information was not available for crediting.

## *Authors*

### IN ORDER OF APPEARANCE

# ALPHABETICALLY

## Introduction

John Clellon Holmes says he named it and it is a jazz term. Jack Kerouac says he started it and it means "beatitude." Norman Mailer traces it all to the cool hipster who went awry. Whatever the beginnings or shadowy meanings, the Fifties will go down in our literary history as the Beat Decade.

Ironically, the attachment of this vivid label is largely due to the double-handed efforts of *Life* and *Time* who, early in the game, picked up the "beats" as the great American rebellion of our youth and our times. This they lampooned in their stylish language of rhetorical deceits. Instead of the anticipated burst balloon, lying limp in the street to be kicked aside into the gutter until the next rebellion came along, "beat" found an echo in our ferocious times and has continued to sound through the nation.

The term lost any significance of meaning, assuming it ever had a specific one, and broke down to a physical type—a kid with beard, rumpled clothes, sandals, bongo drum, jazz records and a copy of *Howl*. Hints of sexual immoralities and use of drugs added a perverted glamor. The "beats"—whether in Venice, California or Greenwich Village, New York—were lumped together in the same mattress on steel spring bed. With more and more name calling came less and less clarity until the word assumed mythic proportions and the Beat Generation had arrived. This might be called typical for America which would rather catalogue people than attempt to understand them.

In titling this book, an obvious dilemma developed which was finally resolved by accepting the popularization as at least readily recognizable even if of questionable pertinence. For the intent here lies beyond the narrow though confused castigations inflicted by ignorant journalists for whom everyone in this gathering is easily labeled as "beat." To the point, the "beats" are those who identify themselves with the ideas of Allen Ginsberg, Jack Kerouac, Gregory Corso and Peter Orlovsky. The others are whatever they might call themselves —"underground," "Black Mountain," "abomunist," or simply poets and writers. There are also the numerous amorphous cliques that tend to cluster around a particular "little" magazine— *Exodus, Big Table, Yugen, Chelsea, Birth,* etc.—or a "little" press—*City Lights, Jargon, Totem, Auerhahn,* etc.

All are Bohemians but all have been labeled as "beat." Certainly it is a different Bohemianism than the cool hipsterism of seven years back, different too from the McCarthy time conformists of ten years ago when almost the only Bohemianism around was that still practiced by the "oldtimers" of the Twenties and Thirties who had never given it up. Possibly the present Bohemians should revel in the popular "beat" label instead of resenting it. This pigeonholing by the soothsayers, whether University academics or Rockerfeller Center journalists, sunders any possible tie of identity with an H-Bomb world of Four Seasons steaks. The cutting of such an umbilical cord establishes the seat of reason and what matters the name calling.

Without presuming to be all-inclusive, the attempt here is to show the new young literary world of New York's Greenwich Village—its writers, its parties, its readings, its *scene*. Before World War II, the Village—then America's only Bohemia—was a vaguely defined geographic area centering around Washington Square, extending north to Fourteenth Street, west to the Hudson River and south to Houston Street. The subsequent housing shortage pushed the young writers in search of inexpensive flats to Chelsea, the East Side, Brooklyn Heights and even further outlaying areas of the city. But the Village is still their haven and center and over ninety per cent of Fred McDarrah's photographs were taken there. The writers, too, who appear here are all "Villagers" or, at least, visitors to this home of Bohemia which has clearly established branches throughout the country especially on the West Coast where the "beat" movement initially started and reached its most outstanding proportions. The selection of contributions attempts to illustrate the chief currents presently evident among these writers.

This Bohemia of social, political and artistic outcasts is deeply rooted in America. Over a hundred years ago, Herman Melville in *Pierre* saluted its presence and perfectly described its qualities: "They are mostly artists of various sorts; painters or sculptors, or indigent students, or teachers of languages, or poets, or fugitive French politicians, or German philosophers. Their mental tendencies, however heterodox at times, are still very fine and spiritual on the whole; since the vacuity of their exchequers leads them to reject the coarse materialism of Hobbes, and incline to the airy exaltations of the Berkleyean philosophy. . . . These are the glorious paupers from whom I learned the profoundest mysteries of things; since their very existence in the midst of such a terrible precariousness of the commonest means of support, affords a problem on which many speculative nut-crackers have been vainly employed. Yet let me offer up three locks of my hair to the memory of all such glorious paupers who have lived and died in this world. Surely, and truly I honor them—noble men often at bottom—and for that very reason I make bold to be gamesome about them; for where fundamental nobleness is, and fundamental honor is due, merriment is never accounted irreverent. The fools and pretenders of humanity, and the imposters and baboons among the gods, these only are offended with raillery. . . ."

Now in the mid-twentieth century, at a time of the country's greatest economic prosperity, has come again the Bohemian discovery of the insignificence of wealth. The Bohemian lives by his ideas and emotions which while easily convertible to money are not then left intact. Poverty, moreover, becomes desireable by freeing a person's attachment to the physical niceties of living beyond, as Walt Whitman said, "the easy dollars that supply the year's plain clothing and meals." This, they would argue, liberates the spirit for the joyful intensities of the human condition.

Accept the idea of the unimportance of money except to provide the necessities and you destroy the foundation of the prevailing American concept of the good life. Neglect wealth, social position and security and you reject the frenzied whirl that has possessed the age. In this social sense, today's Bohemia can be said to be in "revolt" and "revolutionary" with clear political implications. The shape of such politics depends on the emphasis placed on the concept of the role of the individual. There are those for whom the duty is purely personal sensuality and possibly William Burroughs best expresses it. At the other side are those believing the individual to be found only in his life with other people; and here one might place Lawrence Ferlinghetti.

Arguments have been made that the "beats" are neo-fascist in spirit because there is apparent in some of the writings an anti-humanist element, a mystical withdrawel to the inner life, a glorification of individual sensibilities, a denunciation of social responsibilities, use of drugs and the applauding of sexual immorality. It is never possible to avoid this political argument. We have seen in our own time Ezra Pound reading Fascist speeches from Rome and his disciple, John Kasper, leading racist mobs in our southern states; Celine on the side of anti-semitism and the Nazis; Hamsun welcoming Hitler's armies; Hesse's early books—*Steppenwolf* and *Demian*—used cult-like by young SS officers.

Who can question this? But the presence of others must not be forgotten: Sartre and Camus in the French underground, Kenneth Patchen's ardent pacifism, Hemingway's *For Whom the Bell Tolls*, Garcia Lorca murdered in Spain, Auden and Spender—all speaking for the humanistic, democratic spirit.

You can't lump all writers together—not even the Bohemians. And if you mean just the "beats," do you mean *Life* magazine "beat," Ginsberg "beat," Kerouac "beat," or Norman Mailer "beat"? Each should have to be examined separately to make conclusions—whether aesthetic, political or moral. Such variety is the nature of the human; the artist probably more than any other reflects and projects this spectrum of impulses driving people's emotions and thoughts deciding their minds. The writer is no better (though critics think they should be) and no worse (though philosophers tend to allege) than other people. The reader has the choice of agreeing or disagreeing. This is the common ground of all social life and in the field of human expression—of art—there is just as much responsibility for the observer as for the artist. Each has his own and it serves no purpose to state that neither has any, as though that were possible.

Of explicit political attitudes, a deep suspicion and distrust of all state operations and participation dominates a rejection of both armed camps—communist and capitalist. Its configuration is the mushroom shape of the nuclear bomb and the holes dug in the salt mines to circumvent the abolition of national suicide. It spews anti-politics if politics must mean the acceptance of "practical" man hugging shibbeloths of moralities that would countenance non-moral deceits, lies, cheating, distrust, violence, self-agrandissement and national political life aimed at bigger rockets to the moon. If a label is desired, perhaps that of Thoreau is most suited—the Thoreau who envisioned, to alter slightly, "a world at last which can afford to be just to all men, and to treat the individual with respect as a neighbor; which even would not think it inconsistent with its own repose if a few were to live aloof from it, not meddling with it, nor embraced by it, who fulfilled all the duties of neighbors and fellow men. A world which bore this kind of fruit, and suffered it to drop off as fast as it ripened, would prepare the way for a still more perfect and glorious world. . . ."

Along with the rediscovery of the human—the individual—has come the resurgence of poetry as a means of expression. Poetry, assumedly, always functioned this way but the peculiar turn it had taken in America in the previous twenty years had obscured its potency. Poetry had largely become smothered with explication and obscurantism to the extent of poets writing set pieces about minimal fragments of life and reaching a small coterie who alone could decipher the symbols. Prose had fallen into the hands of journalists or literary stylists. Creativity had become tongue-tied by language and art. Walt Whitman's cry was again raised, "What I experience or portray shall go from my composition without a shred of my composition. You shall stand by my side and look in the mirror with me."

The aesthetic problem assumes interest in this current Bohemia in direct relation to the individual writer's view of the role of art. There is the ever-evident denunciation of Academies though in this everchanging Bohemia there are already discernible "schools" forming as aesthete followers group around appointed "leaders." The battles of form vs. content are again waged round the clock and it is questionable if the Ivory Tower of Art is a crushed rubble lying buried off Cape Cod with the radioactive waste of atomic plants. Aesthetic influences range far and wide—Walt Whitman, William Carlos Williams, Ezra Pound—Rimbaud, Apollinaire, Valery—Lorca, Brecht, Mayakovski—Hoelderlin, Smart, Blake —and not only the Western writers but also those of Far East. There are neo-dadaists, neo-surrealists, and neo-romantics. There is no want of aesthetic theories. Contemporary European writers such as Beckett, Ionesco, Genet, and Artaud exert enormous influence. The less well known Americans, Robert Creeley and Charles Olson, are playing an important role in the shaping of current poetics; both were teachers at the avant-garde Black Mountain College, North Carolina, which was forced to close in the early Fifties.

The dominating concern, though, would appear to be more

typically with philosophical questions. This finds particular emphasis in religious quests inextricably bound up in the popular mind with the bursting interest in Zen Buddhism. To Japanese Zen, they look for the ecstasy of experiencing the momentary as against the usual Western view of counting one's enjoyments as pieces of a larger way of life. In Zen, they seek to penetrate beyond the logical aspects of the mind into the core of the human spirit to bring fruition to this "truly human reality."

Alternately, there is the appeal of primitive Christianity—"what Christ really meant"—to which they turn for a humanist, rational, social tradition. In not quite rejecting the nonpurposeful life, they would see in the Sermon on the Mount, the "beatitudes," a pure statement of by what a man should live. This used to be called primitive communism but today is linked more closely with philosophical anarchism. Moreover, God, instead of being dumped, is assuming the proportions of a Revival.

In this litany of influences the atheistic Existentialism developed by Jean Paul Sartre cannot be overlooked especially as it was modified in the writings of Albert Camus. This mixed vision of life, a brew of Zen, Christ, Camus, is clearly reflected in the recent joint statement by Ginsberg, Orlovsky and Corso who sought to define the Beat Generation: ". . . there are six thousand stars at night; but there are billions and billions of unseen stars. Six thousand you can actually count. The sun is a star. But earth isn't a star. You know how many earths can fit into a star, let's say our star the sun? I bet a thousand or more. So there. How does that make you feel? Insignificant? Cheap? Terrible? Envious? Contemptuous? That's why there's a Beat Generation, not because doom hovers over earth manmade doom, doom (destruction) was here before we were born, there's no escape, so why worry about that, destruction is a distraction, there are other things to consider, wondrous things; the Beat Generation is insulted when linked to doom, thoughts of doom, fear of doom, anger of doom. The Beat Generation is because truth rests on the contradictory rattans of the soul. . . . All is endless, limitless, infinity is a dog sitting at its own feet. The BG is a climax, therefore it's as insignificant as anything man can mouth, for what has the BG to do with the dromedaries of the solar system? . . . . Nothing means nothing. Cows, radiator soup, mother's death, war docu-

ments, Alcman's Maiden Song, Greeks wearing shorts, Smith
College; only the wonders of sunset mean anything. . . . Yet
starless things would deprive the BG of its illusions. Why?
Because they, the starless, don't believe in clairvoyant abstrac-
tion, that's why. They really believe that man is, that man
exists, how sad, how absurd! Man does not exist, man is just
an invention of God; a senseless invention in this great movement of insensibility. . . . So don't listen to what earth has to
say, earth is jealous of heaven. Jealous because it knows it's
not even a star. The truth is thick in the fleeted loom. Muti-
nous substance! The truth is deep, the truth is sickening, the
truth is relatively safe; everything but the BG stands amid
the ordeals of lie. . . ."

While Jack Kerouac's novel *On the Road* launched "beat"
in the public eye, it was brought more into focus by Allen
Ginsberg's slim book of poetry, *Howl*. Most academics, university professors, critics and established poets made it ab-
solutely clear what they thought of *Howl*—it stank. In America's literary past, there was another comparable to-do when
Walt Whitman brought out *Leaves of Grass* exactly a hundred years earlier. Ginsberg had William Carlos Williams, the
respected elder of American poets, to champion his cause and
Whitman had Ralph Waldo Emerson who wrote him en-
thusiastically, "I greet you at the beginning of a great career."

Emerson began a one-man crusade for Whitman, sending
copies to his friends and insisting to others that they buy and
read it—"Have you read that wonderful book . . .," he kept
asking.

Now look at the reactions. Charles Eliot Norton acknowl-
edged some good points but ". . . passages of intolerable
coarseness—not gross & licentious, but simply disgustingly
coarse. The book is such, indeed, that one cannot leave it
about for chance readers, and would be very sorry to know
that any woman had looked into it past the title page. . . ."

James Russell Lowell when queried; "No, no, the kind of thing
you describe won't do. When a man aims at originality, he
acknowledges himself consciously unoriginal, a want of self-
respect, etc." J. P. Lesley, friend of Emerson; ". . . had
examined the 'profane and obscene' *Leaves of Grass* and
thought the author a pretentious ass without decency. . . ."

The *Boston Intelligence* roared: "The beastliness of the
author is set forth in his own description of himself, and we

can conceive of no better reward than the lash for such a violation of decency. The author should be kicked from all decent society as below the level of the brute. He must be some escaped lunatic raving in pitiable delirium."

But Emerson stuck with him and Thoreau championed him and Walt Whitman kept on with poetry.

Here are the echoes today. Philip Rahv pronounces, "I have looked over the stuff and it seems pretty vacuous to me." Lionel Trilling: "I have no admiration for the 'beat' literature —except for a few lines or sequences of lines in some of the poems I have read—and my only interest in the whole 'beat' movement is in the quasi-religous aspect of the phenomenon." William Troy: "Any absurdity pushed far enough may lead to a rediscovery of order and grace." Marius Bewly: "I imagine by this time all decent Americans are opposed to fall-out and Eisenhower, but I fail to see why protest against the age should extend to good manners and creased trousers."

Walt Whitman managed through self-effort to sell or give away a thousand or so copies of *Leaves of Grass* in the first few years; *Howl* sold over 50,000 copies in the same span. It had the initial notoriety of a California Court case where local police sought to suppress the City Lights edition. This has largely been forgotten as more recent such cases as *Lady Chatterly's Lover* have taken this public spotlight. But *Howl* keeps selling. Seemingly, every college freshman must be buying it for this ever new and young audience would appear to be the source of continuing readership.

Ferlinghetti's *Coney Island of the Mind* is also having a sensational sale for poetry in America. New Directions, the publishers, have sold tens of thousands and at one time were hard pressed getting copies from the printers to meet the demand. This is extraordinary because a volume of so-called "good" poetry hovers around the 800 sales mark and rarely gets beyond 2,000 except for established poets such as Auden, Moore and Cummings. At University readings, Ginsberg packs thousands into staid halls. In coffee shops throughout the nation, young writers read to a seemingly ever increasing audience. On statistics alone, it is clear that this new literature is speaking for an important part of its generation.

ELIAS WILENTZ

March 1960, Greenwich Village

Allen Ginsberg

I Beg You Come Back & Be Cheerful

*Rummaging through my book shelves one Sunday I came
across a 1950 issue of* Neurotica *magazine and discovered in
it, among other forgotten pieces, a poem by Allen Ginsberg.
A Carroll like nonsense song, it was titled* Fie My Fum. *When
I saw Allen a few days later and asked him about it, he was
delighted at its remembrance and promptly sang it all for me—*
    *Pull my daisy,*
    *Tip my cups,*
    *Cut my thoughts*
    *For coconuts,*
*and so on for three more stanzas. This is the song in the
Robert Frank movie, written by Jack Kerouac, and titled with
the opening line. It struck me as odd—this ten year span—
because I tended to think of Allen's writings as all of very
recent vintage and forgotten that he had been hard at it for
quite some time. Even* Howl *is now more than five years old.*

Tonite I got hi in the window of my apartment
        chair at 3 AM
gazing at Blue incandescent torches
        bright-lit street below
clotted shadows looming on a new laid pave
—as last week Medieval rabbiz
            plodded thru the brown raw
            dirt turned over—sticks
                & cans
        and tired ladies sitting on spanish
            garbage pails—in the deadly heat
              —one month ago
            the fire hyrants were awash—
        the sun at 3 P.M. today in a haze—
now all dark outside, a cat crosses
        the street silently—I meow
and she looks up, and passes a
            pile of rubble on the way
        to a golden shining garbage pail
            (phosphor in the night
                & alley stink)
            (or door-can mash)
          —Thinking America is a chaos
Police clog the streets with their anxiety,
        Prowl cars creak & halt:

Today a woman, 20, slapped her brother
            playing with his infant bricks—
        toying with a huge rock—
            "Don't do that now! the cops! the cops!"
        And there was no cop there—
            I looked around my shoulder—
        a pile of crap in the opposite direction.

Tear gas! Dynamite! Mustaches!
I'll grow a beard and carry lovely
        bombs,
I will destroy the world, slip in between
        the cracks of death
    And change the Universe—Ha!
I have the secret, I carry
        Subversive salami in
                my ragged briefcase
"Garlic, Poverty, a will to Heaven,"
    a strange dream in my meat:

Radiant clouds, I have heard God's voice in
        My sleep, or Blake's awake, or my own or
the dream of a delicatessen of snorting cows
        and bellowing pigs—
            The chop of a knife
        a finger severed in my brain—
            a few deaths I know—

    O brothers of the Laurel
Is the world real?
        Is the Laurel
a joke or a crown of thorns?—

            Fast, pass
            up the ass
            Down I go
            Cometh Woe

—the street outside,
    me spying on New York.
The dark truck passes snarling &
    vibrating deep—

What
    if
        the
            worlds
            were
            a
              series
                    of steps

                        What
                        if
                        the
                        steps
              joined
        back
      at
    the
Margin

Leaving us flying like birds into Time
    —the eyes and car headlights—
    or senses—The shrinkage of emptiness
in the Nebulae

These Galaxies cross like pinwheels & they pass
    like gas—
What forests are born.

Jonathan Williams

Robert Nichols
Kenward Elmslie
Marvin Cohen
Kenneth Koch
Richard Davidson
Jonathan Williams

*The winds which passed over my dwelling were such as sweep over the ridges of mountains, bearing the broken strains, or celestial parts only, of terrestial music. The morning wind forever blows, the poem of creation is uninterrupted; but few are the ears that hear it. Olympus is but the outside of the earth everywhere.*

*Henry Thoreau*

ROBERT NICHOLS

*Mother*

Mother come back. I'm getting a complex without you. I fear I am not an *homme du monde*. There is so much about life I don't know. Take just the everyday things, I am almost submerged by them.

Mother I need your advice about the baby. Does it have diaper rash? Should it still be sucking its thumb at this age?

Mother, my wife is spending too much money. She has charge accounts in eighteen department stores. This is something I cannot discuss even with my best friends.

Mother, there are so many pleasant, happy things I want to talk over with you.

Mother, why did you ever move to Miami Beach anyway? Won't you come to visit us here in Seattle? I promise not to interfere in your personal life in any way.

Mother. I want you to know I haven't forgotten my dream. Did I tell you I'd taken up the harmonica again? I've learned to tell stories in dialect. I can clean spark plugs.

Mother I haven't an Oedipus, really I haven't. I'm just sick of my peer group. I'm longing for the sight of a few grey hairs.

Mother why are all you people from the Twenties so suspicious?

Mother we need a baby sitter. I'm having trouble sleeping. I wasn't cut out to be an account executive. You know I always hated to wear shoes.

Mother do you remember when I played Peter Pan? I jumped out of the library window onto the cretonne sofa? I had wings then.

Mother do you remember nursing me when I was sick? The curtains are drawn. I look up and watch you feeding me Milk of Magnesia from a big spoon. I feel you stroking my forehead with your cool hands, like an angel.

Mother, where is that recipe for brownies you promised us three years ago?

Mother, have you forgotten? Mother. Mother. Mother.

Mother, I miss you. I need you. Don't you miss me too? Mother do you love me? Honestly, I don't mean any harm. I'm just a sweet guy. I want to gab about old times.

Marvin Cohen

Kenward Elmslie

MARVIN COHEN
*Prose Poem*

I woke up feeling too good to be true. That was my first mistake.

I yawned, and with powerful ease of breath blew the ceiling away from my bedroom, until the lady upstairs fell on me with violent curiosity of desire.

I married her next day to facilitate our growing friendship. It was a marriage of convenience, since she was intolerably wealthy and I was sufficiently poor.

She made me move upstairs. We cooked our meals by rubbing our bodies together while holding the raw meat and vegetables. It was amazingly effective. Animal heat, as yet unexploited, contains unlimited possibilities as a source of energy. We thought of selling ourselves to the government: But that would be prostitution.

This story ends, though, sadly: We loved each other to extinction. Even our graves are invisible.


KENWARD ELMSLIE
*Families in Iowa*

Dad's crewcut wig smelled of candies.
Son said hug me here, hi pal, voom gee good.
Then Niece fell from the glassed-in crisper
"beset by the junebug plague"—namely Uncle.
Down at the incinerator Nephew exposed himself
But Auntie was licking whips in the silo,
Whips named Sis. The Twins finished their baby-shaped
Popsicle and Cousin and Brother rubbed and rubbed
Against Granny's earache. How mossy, she wept.

Bye now, Mother announced. And so everyone left for institutions,
Stadiums, subways, mountains and many such zany palaces.
Mother unzipped and out leapt Mom Mummy and Mammy
And together those four drove
To the experimental cemetary
To have fun.

KENNETH KOCH

from a long poem—*Lunch*

We stood in the little hutment in Biarritz
Waiting for lunch, and your hand clasped mine
And I felt it was sweaty;
And then lunch was served,
Like the bouquet of an enchantress.
Oh the green whites and red yellows
And purple whites  of lunch!

The bachelor eats his lunch,
The married man eats his lunch,
And old Uncle Joris belches
The seascape in which a child appears
Eating a watermelon and holding a straw hat.
He moves his lips as if to speak
But only sea air emanates from this childish beak.
It is the moment of sorrows,
And in the shores of history,
Which stretch in both directions, there are no happy tomorrows.
But Uncle Joris holds his apple up and begins to speak
To the child. Red waves fan my universe with the green macaw of
    lunch.

This street is deserted;
I think my eyes are empty;
Let us leave
Quickly.
Day bangs on the door and is gone.

Then they picked him up and carried him away from that company.
When he awoke he was in the fire department, and sleepy but not
    tired.

They gave him a hoseful of blue Spain to eat for lunch,
And Portugal was waiting for him at the door, like a rainstorm
   of evening raspberries.

It is time to give lunch to my throat and not my chest.
What? either the sting ray has eaten my lunch
Or else—and she searches the sky for something else;
But I am far away, seeming blue-eyed, empirical . . .

Let us give lunch to the lunch—
But how shall we do it?
The headwaiters expand and confer;
Will little pieces of cardboard box do it.
And what about silver and gold pellets?
The headwaiters expand and confer:

And what if the lunch should refuse to eat anything at all?
Why then we'd say be damned to it,
And the red doorway would open on a green railway
And the lunch would be put in a blue car
And it would go away to Whippoorwill Valley
Where it would meet and marry Samuel Dogfoot, and bring forth
    seven offspring,
All of whom would be half human, half lunch;
And when we saw them, sometimes, in the gloaming,
We would take off our mining hats and whistle Tweet twee-oo.
With watering mouths staring at the girls in pink organdy frocks,
Not realizing they really were half edible,
And we would die still without knowing it;
So to prevent anything happening that terrible
Let's give everybody we see and like a good hard bite right now,
To see what they are, because it's time for lunch!

RICHARD DAVIDSON

*Moon Over McDougal Street*

## HE
Do you love me way out man and so cool. . . .

## SHE
I love you. This is absolute truth, isn't it Johnny?
I mean this is everything. Who can be interested
in anything else today?

When I was born and born I was
Into life as secure as a rug
And I lived in a nice
house
And it was a white house
And it stood on a street so wide and grim
And it bloomed like a flower in the summer
And the leaves opened wide their ironic
grin

And the sun beat down and my father strong
and he loved me with a briefcase love
And he told me how to behave in society
And my life as secure as a rug

And then the yells from the sky above and I knew
I had to go
On and on the waters spent
I didn't know where I went
I just had to row the boat.

Oh the sun beat down and the world turned green
And the lights blew up the evening air
And I found myself on McDougal Street
And I was so pure and debonair

Then I saw him and he burned up my eyes
And he told me that I was his eternal truth.
And he was a dark bright boy
And he was a lonely boy
And his beard rubbed against my untouched chin
And we bloomed like a flower in the summer
And the leaves opened wide their ironic grin

What care I. Confirmation's gone and my parents can go to hell
On and on we drove the storm
Back into the time we both were born
And our ship rocked in the sea.
Oh the sun beat down and I was high
And my love burned like a midnight star
And we both knew quite suddenly we said
We didn't know where we were.

And it was darkness.
And it was pain
And he broke the walls of my careful heart
And we trudged against the sidewalks of the city
And our dreams so carefully torn apart.

Oh the sun beat down and alone am I
Barefooted without eternal truth
And the earth slides by like a nightmare
With a scalpel in its tooth.

Oh to be free and to act so free
Oh God, where are the stars above
And what is my name in the soul of night
Oh God, is there really love?

JONATHAN WILLIAMS
*Over A Beer with Fielding Dawson*


you know the guy you never sent a copy of *Ajax* to,
you know, Gene Reid ('Cyclone') . . . ?

well, he got killed the other day in that crash,
off Bermuda

I looked at my friend, Cyclone's
best friend. What a time it is here, man, he said.

Jay Zoos!

yet it is a month later the news really gets at me, via
Poe's *Domain of Arnheim,* Delius's *Appalachia,*
and the paintings of Arthur B. Davies and
George Caleb Bingham . . .

> ("And echoes swell across the mighty stream,
>     Ah!")

and tho making it up, emoting from the far-off mountain,
Cyclone, St. Louis, Missouri, the 1950's,
still seem to mean the Huckleberry Finn Scene, again:

"I am a Sotherne man," languid amid
rivers, on rafts . . .

except nowadays
All-American Boys become

ensigns

of very American domain, where hurricanes
kill cyclones

Fielding Dawson

A party at The Living Theatre given by Jonathan Williams, publisher of Jargon Books, to celebrate the appearance of "Red Carpet for the Sun" by the Canadian poet Irving Layton

Jonathan Williams

Frank O'Hara
Joel Oppenheimer

James Grady
Seymour Krim

Irving Layton

Edward Dahlberg, novelist

Frank O'Hara reading with Ray Bremser, LeRoi Jones and Allen Ginsberg at a benefit for Totem Press

Frank O'Hara

Personal Poem
Poem

*Frank O'Hara lives in the Village but works midtown at the Museum of Modern Art and nearly every time I've seen him he's been neatly dressed in a suit and white shirt and tie. I've been told that he writes some of his poems while on his lunch break in that Fifties and Fifth Avenue horrendous maze of glass, aluminum and steel. And undoubtedly they reflect it somewhat. But in the intricate patterns which he develops and interweaves there is a great subtlety of feeling which becomes particularly apparent when you hear him read the poems aloud.*

*Personal Poem*

Now when I walk around at lunchtime
I have only two charms in my pocket
an old Roman coin Mike Kanemitsu gave me
and a bolt-head that broke off a packing case
when I was in Madrid the others never
brought me too much luck though they did
help keep me in New York against coercion
but now I'm happy for a time and interested

I walk through the luminous humidity
passing the House of Seagram with its wet
and its loungers and the construction to
the left that closed the sidewalk if
I ever get to be a construction worker
I'd like to have a silver hat please
and get to Moriarty's where I wait for
Leroi and hear who wants to be a mover and
shaker the last five years my batting average
is .016 that's that, and Leroi comes in
and tells me Miles Davis was clubbed 12
times last night outside BIRDLAND by a cop
a lady asks us for a nickel for a terrible
disease but we don't give her one we
don't like terrible diseases, then

we go eat some fish and some ale it's
cool but crowded we don't like Lionel Trilling
we decide, we like Don Allen we don't like
Henry James so much we like Herman Melville
we don't want to be in the poets' walk in
San Francisco even we just want to be rich
and walk on girders in our silver hats
I wonder if one person out of the 8,000,000 is
thinking of me as I shake hands with Leroi
and buy a strap for my wristwatch and go
back to work happy at the thought possibly so
it would probably be only the one person
who gave me a blue whistle from a crackerjack box.

*Poem*


Khrushchev is coming on the right day!
                                        the cool graced light
is pushed off the enormous glass piers by hard wind
and everything is tossing, hurrying on up
                              this country
has everything but *politesse,* a Puerto Rican cab driver says
and five different girls I see
                        look like Piedie Gimbel
with her blonde hair tossing too,
                              as she looked when I pushed
her little daughter on the swing on the lawn it was also windy

last night we went to a movie and came out,
                                  Ionesco is greater
than Becket, Vincent said, that's what I think, blueberry blintzes
and Khrushchev was probably being carped at
                              in Washington, no *politesse*
Vincent tells me about his mother's trip to Sweden
                                    Hans tells us
about his father's life in Sweden, it sounds like Grace Hartigan's
painting *Sweden*
                  so I go home to bed and names drift through my head
Purgatorior Merchado, Gerhard Schwartz and Gaspar Gonzalez, all
      unknown figures of the early morning as I go to work

where does the evil of the year go
                              when September takes New York
and turns it into ozone stalagmites
                              deposits of light
                              so I get back up
make coffee, and read François Villon, his life, so dark
      New York seems blinding and my tie is blowing up the street
I wish it would blow off
                              though it is cold and somewhat warms my neck
as the train bears Khrushchev on to Pennsylvania Station
      and the light seems to be eternal
      and joy seems to be inexorable
      I am foolish enough always to find it in wind

Roberts Blossom, poet and playwright

LeRoi Jones
John Fles
Bruce Fearing
Paul Blackburn
Diane Di Prima
Tuli Kupferberg

*I placed his desk close up to a small side-window, a window
which originally had afforded a lateral view of certain grimy
backyards and bricks, but which, owing to subsequent erec-
tions, commanded at present no view at all, though it gave
some light. Within three feet of the panes was a wall and the
light came down from far above, between two loft buildings,
as from an opening in a dome.*

*Herman Melville*

Jack Stamm, poet and translator from the Japanese

Hazel Ford, poet

LeROI JONES

*Epistrophe*
(*for yodo*)

It's such a static reference; looking
out the window all the time! the eyes' limits ...
On good days, the sun.

& what you see. (here in New York)
Walls and buildings; or in the hidden gardens
of opulent Queens: profusion, endless stretches of leisure.

It's like being chained to some dead actress;
& she keeps trying to tell you something horribly maudlin.

e.g.
      ("the leaves are flat & motionless.")

What I know of the mind
seems to end here;
Just outside my face.

I wish some weird looking animal
would come along.

JOHN FLES

*morning poem*

its hard for me to adjust to weather
Im still wearing my goddam summer clothes in fall

this morning, for instance, my legs were numb
(the cold produced some nice dreams during the night tho)
I had just one blanket on the bed

suddenly winters falling on us
                    like a hunk of ice
Im not prepared

OR I go out dressed warm and the day is hot
I wish they would make up their mind

anyway, lying in bed in the morning, like this morning
I have the radio nestled close to my head (right in the bed)
to reach out, still in sleep, the knob . . .
the Masterwork Hour (Carlo Chavez & Hector Villa-Lobos)

a poet would call this the edge of a season
an academic: a period of transition

                    bless you all
                    I hope you dont have as much trouble as I do

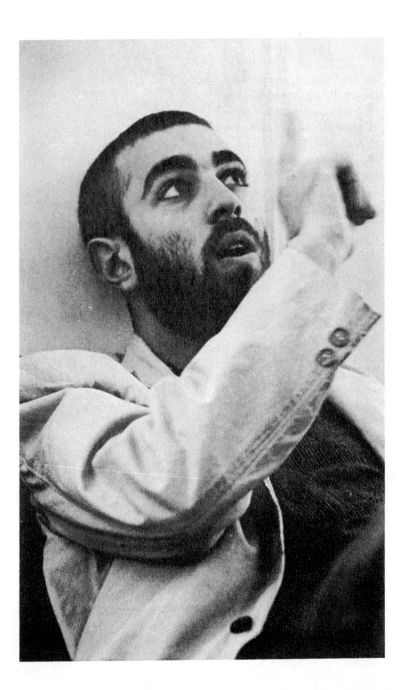

BRUCE FEARING

*Some Brown Sparrows*

Some brown sparrows who live
in the Bronx Zoo visit often
the captive Victoria Crested
Pheasant, visit captive Peacocks,
Cockatoos. They fly through bars
to visit also monkeys, jackals,
bears. They delouse themselves in
cage dust, shaking joyously;
they hunt for bread crumbs, seeds
or other tidbits. Briefly,
they lead free sparrow lives
and fly free.

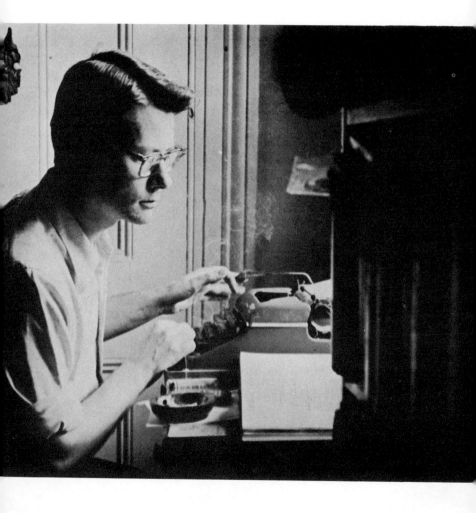

PAUL BLACKBURN

*The Needle*

Two blocks away
     night traffiic goes whipping through
     the avenue          the fast motors

It's not as though one could see it
It's not as though nothing were good

     Even above the rooftops
     stars are mixed with cloud
     Only the brightest get through

The absolute bureaucracy of size and closeness
     which coefficient is power

But the cat crosses the tiled roof at this hour
               in the dark night
                  in the moon

DIANE DI PRIMA

from *Necrophilia*

the highbridge body, roach, walks
on thin legs
limps slightly; dreamsweat makes acid
my pajamas; the sheet moves
with your breathing

light
dapples the ceiling, undermines the
walls; (cars pass); the child
stirs, but she does not cry;
wind climbs the fire escape and shakes the window
    knees
    rise
    and
    fall

in this new york, cell on monastic
cell, they sleep, we sleep; dreams
stream from the women's hair;
the highbridge roach
walks
where the kitchen was;
ice claws the windows, wind
unlocks the door

how many nights shall I lie at your side
wearing pajamas; using a separate
pillow

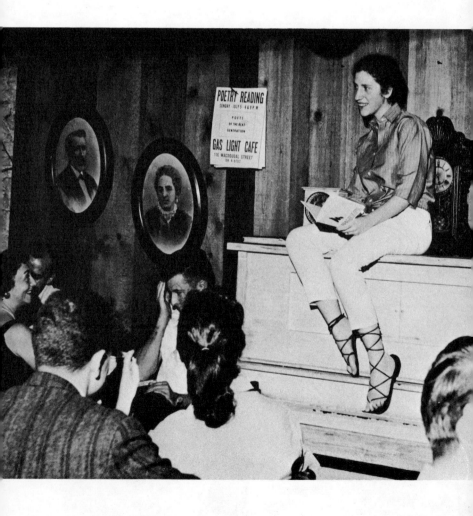

TULI KUPFERBERG

*Greenwich Village of My Dreams*

A rose in a stone.
Chariots on the West Side Highway.
Blues in the Soviet Union.
Onions in times square.
A Japanese in Chinatown.
A soup sandwich.
A Hudson terraplane.
Chess in a Catskill bungalow.
Awnings in Atlanta.
Lewisohn stadium in the blackout.
Brooklyn beneath the East River.
     the waves passover.
The Battery in startling sunlight.
Kleins in Ohrbachs.
Love on the dole, Roosevelt not elected.
Hoover under the 3rd Ave El
Joe Gould kissing Maxwell Bodenheim
     & puffing on his pipe
Edna Millay feeling Edmund Wilson
Charlie Parker & Ted Joans talking
     in Sheridan Sq Park & its cold man!
The Cedar St Bar with Cedars in it
     & autos crashing against the cedars
The Chase Manhattan Bank closed
     down for repairs. To open as the
     new Waldorf Cafeteria.
Lionel Trilling kissing Allen Ginsberg
     after great Reading in the Gaslight
The Limelight changes its name to
     the Electric Light & features
     Charlie Chaplin as a s(w)inging
     waiter
Edgar Allan Poe becoming the dentist
     in the Waverly dispensary & giving
     everyone free nitrous oxide high

Louis getting thrown out of Louis'
San Remo stepping up to the bar &
      asking for a wet Martini
The Charleston on Charles St
      featuring my Sister Eileen
      & the Kronstadt sailors.
Max Eastman & John Reed
      buying Gungawala hashish candy
      at the German Delicatessen on 6th
      Ave & West 4th Street.
Tourists bringing pictures to sell
      to artists in their annual disposition.
Civilians telling cops to move on
Coffeehouses that sell brandy
      in their coffee cups
Eugene O'Neill insisting on coffee
John Barrymore in offbroadway Hamlet
Walt Whitman cruising on MacDougal
Ike & Mamie drunk in Minettas
Khrushchev singing peat bog soldiers
      in the circle (with a balalaika)
Everybody kissing & hugging squeezing
Khrushchev & Eisenhower a big fat kiss
The world an art
Life a joy
The village come to life again

I wake up singing
I that dwell in New York
Sweet song bless my mouth
Beauty bless my eyes

        *Song of the world*
        *Fly forth from dreams!*

How beautiful is love
And the fruit thereof
Holy holy holy
A kiss and a star

John Fles

Irving Rosenthal, Editor of "Big Table" One

Jonas Mekas, film critic of "Village Voice"

George Preston, founder of Artist's Studio, with Robert Lasoda
and friend

Philip Lamantia and Kirby Doyle visiting from San Francisco

Stanley Fisher, artist and teacher

At the studio of David Lambert, musician

Seymour Krim
Making It!

*I was supposed to meet Krim at a party but he never showed up; then three days later he sought me out. He couldn't get there that night, he apologized in his peculiarly intense manner, his shoulders hunched as though he were a football player about to make a line plunge. And as explanation he waved his right hand which was in an enormous plaster cast. We finally did get together for lunch and this time there was another Krim behind those large round eye glasses—joking, jovial, laughing. We talked about his* White Cadillac *piece that had just come out in* Exodus *magazine and I was amazed how willing he was to speak critically about his writings. I never did find out how he broke his hand.*

When has an inside phrase like "making it" or so-and-so's "got it made" shot with such reality through the museum of official English? In this terse verbal shorthand lies a philosophy of life that puts a gun in the back of Chase Manhattan rhetoric and opens up, like a money-bag, the true values that make the Sammys and Susies of modern city life run today. *You've got it made.* How the words sing a swift jazz poem of success, hi-fi, the best chicks (or guys), your name in lights, pot to burn, jets to L. A. and London, bread in the bank, baby, and a fortress built around your ego like a magic suit of armor! *You've got it made.* Royalties pouring in, terraces stretching out, hip movie starlets strutting in butt-parade, nothing but Jack Daniels with your water, your name in Skolsky's column, Tennessee for lunch, dinner with—somebody who swings, sweetheart! And tomorrow the world (as a starter).

Middle-class ideals of success once curled the lip of the intellectual; today he grins not, neither does he snide. Columbia professor, poet, painter, ex-Trotskyite, one-shot New Yorker satirist, Partisan Review editor—they all live in the same world for a change and that world says, go! The Marxist, neo-Christian, romantic, humanitarian values of 20 years ago are great for the mind's library and its night-time prayer mat; but will they fill the cancerous hunger in the soul for getting what *you* want? Softies become tough, toughies get harder, men dig that they'd rather be women, women say to hell with lilacs and become men, the road gets rougher (as Frankie lays his Kiplingish message on us) and you've got to move, hustle, go for the ultimate broke or you'll be left with a handful of nothing, Jack and Jill! What happened to the world out *there,* the one you always thought you loved and honestly - couldn't - get - enough - of - without - wanting - a - sou - in - return for your pure and holy feelings? *Baby, that world went up in the cornball illusions of yesterday! Forget it just like it never knew you were alive. This bit about being a fine writer, a dedicated actor, a movie-maker with Modern Museum notions of heaven, a musician because you truly love it, a painter because you die when you smell the color? Don't make me laugh—it's not good for the stitches, dad. This world (nuts, this rutting universe!) is a Mt. Everest, kiddo, and you've got to start climbing now or the dumbwaiter of this age will slam you down into the black basement. Use whatever you've got and use what you* ain't *got, too!*

Throughout the jumping metropolis of New York one sees vertical fanaticism, the Thor-type upward thrust of the entire being, replacing pale, horizontal, mock-Christian love of fellow-creature; the man or woman who is High Inside, hummingly self-aware, the gunner and the gunnerette in the turret of the aircraft that is Self, is watching out for number one with a hundred new-born eyes. He or she has been slicked down by the competition to a lean, lone-eagle, universe-supporting role. Hey Atlas, did you ever think that common man and woman would be imprisoned under the burden of your heroic weight and find it the ultimate drag rather than the ultimate god-like stance, without value, nobility or purpose? The ancient symphonies of Man have lost their meaning. It is hopelessness that drives the modern whirlwind striver to put such emphasis on personal achievement.

In every brain-cell of intellectual and artistic life the heat is on in America today no differently than it is in business. Values? Purpose? Selectivity? Principles. *For the birds,*

*Charley! I want to make it and nothing's going to stand in my
way because everything is crap except making it! Be honest,
for Godsakes. I want my ego to ride high, my heart to bank the
loot of life, my apartment to swing, my MG to snarl down the
highway, my pennant to wave above the scattered turds of
broken dreams for a better world! Why don't you level and
say you want the same, you hypocrite?*

With the blessings of psychiatry, enlightened (so-called)
selfishness has become the motto of hip city life; the once-
Philistine is admired for his thick skin and wallet; the poor
slob who translates Artaud but can't make his rent, a girl,
or hold his own at a party is used as a dart-board for the wit
of others—not by the "enemy," either, but by his very Village
brothers who have forsaken a square idealism for a bite-
marked realism. The only enemy today is failure, failure, failure, and the only true friend is—success! How? In what line?
Whoring yourself a little? Buttering up, sucking up, self-sales-
manship, the sweet oh-let-me-kiss-your-ass-please smile? *Don't
be naive, friend. You think this hallucinated world is the moon-
light sonata or something? You think anyone cares about your
principles or (don't make me puke!) integrity or that they
make the slightest ripple in the tempest of contemporary
confusion? Go sit at home, then, you plastic saint and keep
pure like the monks with your hands on your own genitalia!
Because if you want to make it out in the world, baby, you
have to swing, move, love what you hate and love yourself
for doing it, too!*

The one unforgivable sin in city life today is not to *make
it*. Even though the cush of success may seem hollow to the
victor as his true self sifts the spoils, alone and apart from
the madding cats who envy him, he knows that his vulnerable
heart could not bear the pain of being a loser. Wasn't success
drummed at him every day, in every way, in relation to

women, status, loot—Christ, the image of himself in his own eyes? Didn't he see those he admired in his tender years flicked off like so many flies because they'd never made a public victory of their talents? My God, man, what else could he do except be a success (or kill himself)—the world being what it is?

For *making it* today has become the only tangible value in an environment quaking with insecurity and life's mockery of once-holy goals, which the bored witch of modern history has popped over the rim of the world for sport, like an idle boy with paper pellets. *How can you buy grand abstractions of human brotherhood for that daily fix needed by your ego when Dostoievsky and Freud have taught us we hate our parents, brothers, sisters and wives, as well as friends? Oh, no, you can't snow us, you peddlers of fake hope! We know you for what you are: vaseline-tongued frustrates who wanted to make it and lost. Man, how the wound shows behind your your pathetic rationalizations!*

The paddled values and euphemisms of a more leisurely time have been ruthlessly stripped away under the hospital light of today's world; honesty, integrity, truthfulness, seem sentimental hangovers from a pastoral age, boy-scout ideals trying to cope with an armored tank of actuality that is crumpling the music-box values of the past like matchsticks. It is not Truth that is pertinent today, in the quaint dream of some old philosopher; it is the specific truths of survival, getting, taking, besting, as the old order collapses like a grounded parachute around the stoney vision of the embittered modern adult. *What is left but me? mutters the voice of reality, and how else can I save myself except by exhausting every pore in the race with time?* We see in America today a personal ambition unparalled in fierce egocentricity, getting ahead, achieving the prize, making a score—for the redemption of self. Are the ends good? Does it matter to the world? Will it pass muster at the gates of judgment? *Such questions are ridiculous: they presume a God above man rather than the god of life who thumps within my chest for more, faster, bigger, conquests for me, me, ME!*

As the individual stands his lonely vigil in the polar night of the desolation of all once agreed-upon values—as they have receded like the tide, rolling back into the past—where else, he cries, can he turn but to his own future? Who else will help him? What can he or she do but mount the top of personal fulfillment in a world that has crumbled beneath the foot? Upon the neon-lit plains of the modern city comes the tortured cry of a million selves for a place in the sun of personal godhood. As one by one the lights of the old-fashioned planets Peace, Love, Happiness, have flickered and gone out, plunging all into the spook jazzglow of a new surrealist dawn, the only believable light comes from the soul-jet of need that burns in the private heart. *Let the lousy world crash like a demented P-38! What can I do about it? I'm a pawn of this age like you. Man, my only escape-hatch is making it at the highest pitch I can dream of!*

An individualism just short of murder has replaced the phantom of socialism as the idols of the recent past shrink into mere trophies on the mocking walls of history. In an existence so dream-like, uncertain, swift, the only nailed-down values that remain are those that can be seen in the bank-book of life. *Can honors be taken away from me? Fame? Money? The beauty I can possess (by name or dollar) in both flesh and leather? No! Don't croon to me of art or soul in a world that has flipped loose from its moorings, seen the futility of truth, the platitude of spiritual hope, the self-deception in innocence, the lack of discrimination in goodness, the pettiness of tears! You live only once, Jack, and if you don't swing with the fractured rhythms of this time—if you hide behind the curtains of a former, simpler, child's world of right and wrong—you condemn yourself to the just sneers of those who dig the real world as it is! Baby, there is no significance today but* you, *and the sooner you wake up to the full horror of this fact, the better!*

By time-honored esthetic and moral standards the knowing modern man, and woman, is a barely polite gangster; his machine-gun is his mind, ideas his bullets, power and possession his goals. The reduction of the real to the usable has been whittled into a necessity by the impossible number of potential choices within himself: he knows, after juggling more thoughts than he can reach conclusions about, that he must snap down the lid on fruitless speculation and use the precious energy for making warheads on the spears of practicality. Victims of their own subjective desperation, pigmies under the heavens of thought that dot the roof of their minds with a million perverse stars, converge upon the external prizes of life like hordes released from prison: eager to bury the freedom of the mind's insanity in the beautiful sanity of— making it! *Yes, yes, I will convert the self that bugs me into an objective victory in the steel and weighable world! I will take the scalding steam of my spirit and hiss it outward like an acetylene torch upon the hard shale of life, and cut diamonds for myself! You say this therapy of mine adds brutality to the soul of modernity, that I care only for my private need at the expense of the world? That my fuel is desperation and that I'm marvellously indifferent about adding my shot of cruel self-interest to an already amoral environment? I don't deny it. Survival at its highest conception* means *making it! To live you must conquer if you're normal enough to hate being stuck with your futile being and smart enough to know you must trade it for success!*

*For what else is there? Dying at parties, as I used to, when I saw some headliner bring the fawn out of even the best people, who swooned around this living symbol of magic?*

*Eating my heart out because I didn't have the admiration, the*
*chicks, the loot, the* attention *I and all human beings demand*
*out of life? Suppose I do know how cheap and unlike my orig-*
*inal ideal it all is? You want it too, you envious bastard, you*
*know you do. Spit it out that the ego is the world today for*
*all of us and that without its gratification living is a hell, a*
*roasting on the skewer of frustration as you watch others*
*grab the nooky! Jack, life is too far gone—too man-eat-man—*
*for your wistful moralizing and pansy references to the cathe-*
*drals of the past. It's only the present that counts in a world*
*that has no forseeable future, and I'm human enough to want*
*to swing my way to the grave—sweetheart, you can have*
*immortality!*

In an age that has seen the abandonment, because they are
too costly, of cherished political and personal hopes, hypo-
dermic realism inside and business-like efficiency outside becomes the new style. The address-book replaces the soul,
doing is the relief of being, talking of thinking, getting of
feeling. *I've got to numb myself in action, exhaust this inner*
*fiend, or else all the hopelessness of this so-called life of mine*
*will come bursting through its trap-door and overwhelm me!*
*I've got to swing, plan, plot, connive, go and get and get*
*some more, because what else is there, Buster?* The frenzied
tempo of achievement is matched only by the endless desert
within; the futility-powered desperado drives himself ever for-
ward, trying to find in action some publicly-applauded significance that is freezingly absent in solitude. Does it matter that
he finds his buddies who have made it as rocket-desperate and
unsatisfied as himself?

*Hell no. Doesn't the world admire us and isn't it obvious*
*that it's better to be miserable as a storm-trooper than as a*
*Jew? Wasn't my picture in Look, wasn't I on Mike Wallace's*
*show and didn't I turn down an invitation from Long John?*
*Doesn't my answering-service hum with invitations, haven't*

*I made it with that crazy-looking blonde who sings at the Persian Room as well as that distinguished lady novelist who lives near Dash Hammett's old apartment on West 10th? Don't I jive with Condon as well as Wystan Auden, Jim Jones (when he's in town) as well as Maureen Stapelton, Bill Zeckendorf, Bill Rose, Bill Styron, Bill Faulkner, Bill Basie, Bill Williams, Bill deKooning, Bill Holden—just on the Bill front? Don't I get tips on the market, complimentary copies of Big Table as well as Holiday, didn't I put down Dali at that party for being square and get a big grin from Adlai Stevenson for doing so?*

*Man, I know what I'm doing! I'm swinging instead of standing still, I'm racing with a racing age, I'm handling 17 things at once and I'm scoring with them all! Life's too wild today, sonny, to worry about the fate of the race or private morality or nun-like delicacies of should-I or should-I-not; anyone with brains or even imagination is a self-driven marauder with the wisdom to know that if he hustles hard enough he can have a moat full of gravy and a penthouse-castle high over life's East River! I'm bartering my neuroses for AT&T (not crying over them to Beethoven's Ninth like you, you fake holy man!) and bemoaning my futile existence with Mumm's Extra Dry and the finest hemp from Laredo and my new Jackson Pollock and my new off-Broadway hump and my new book and my new play and my new pad and this TV show they're gonna build around me and—Jesus, I've got it made!*

. . . . while down below the lusting average man and woman sweats in jealousy at the sight of these dexodrene angels, the very inspiration of what he and she can become if only they, too, can put that last shred of shame behind them and swing, extrovert yourself, get with it, make that buck, make that chick, make that poem, make this crazy modern scene *pay off*, O my heart, so I too can sink my teeth in the sirloin and wear the pearls of hell!

A party at The Judson Gallery announcing
a new issue of "Exodus" magazine

Paul Blackburn with Sarah and Lee Ann Golden

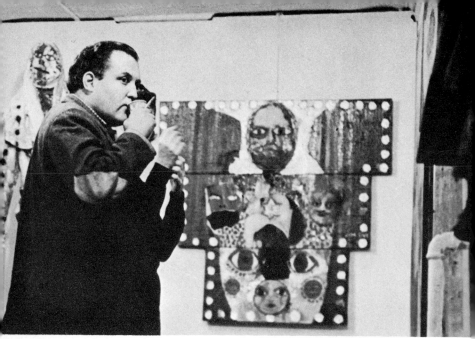

Jock Livingston, actor and critic  Painters Peter Forakis, Richard Tyler and Deanne Dexter

Marc Ratcliff, art director of "Exodus,"
Howard Moody, Minister of Judson Memorial Church

William Morris reading in Washington Square Park. He was arrested once by the police for reading in the Park but the Judge dismissed the case.

Lenore Jaffee
Robert Creeley
Brigid Murnaghan
Dan Propper
James Grady
Sally Stern
William Morris

*I used to think that I could imagine all passions, all feelings, all states of the heart and mind; but how little did I know what it is to be mingled with another's being! Thou only hast taught me that I have a heart—thou only hast thrown a deep light downward, and upward, into my soul. Thou only hast revealed me to myself; for without thy aid, my best knowledge of myself would have been merely to know my own shadow—to watch it flickering on the wall, and mistake its fantasies for my own actions.*

*Nathaniel Hawthorne*

LENORE JAFFEE

*Mr. T and his friends*

One by one
I met, selected
the members of my coterie, my clan.

Nothing within reason was too much to do for any of them, for all
brought love
and were given like for like with smiling grace . . .

until one night,
wearying . . .
not knowing whom to love the best
I sent away all
into the long corridors of the city . . .

not quite knowing why

perhaps that they might vie with one another
in ways to win back my love . . .

but now they are hanging about in uncomfortable fashion
and I am none
the gladder for any of this

I shall soon take up residence elsewhere.

ROBERT CREELEY

*The Gift*

He hands
down the gift
as from a great
height, his

precious
understanding clothed
in miraculous
fortitude. This

is the present
of the ages, all
rewards
in itself

But the lady—
she, disdain-
ful, all
in white for

this occasion—cries
out petulantly, is
that all, is
that all, is
that all.

BRIGID MURNAGHAN

*Daisy*

Why don't you wear a daisy in
       your hair . . .
Instead of one of those hothouse flowers.

A daisy soon dies out of water
All the daisies in the city are
       hothouse anyway.

When I see daisies I want to see
      a field covered
So I can stretch out and know if
    they were picked they'd be
  dead in an hour.

Paint me a daisy to wear in my hair
If you're right it will have the
Look of my beautiful child!!!

Reading at the International Cafe

DAN PROPPER

*Afternoon*

Asleep
you are a different person:
the chinablue-eyed
Modigliani-long-hot-catlike
you
relaxes
into a womanshadowed girl,
warm, curled-up,
the soft sigh of your breath
issuing . . .

I stand
over your bed
—I want to gently embrace
your tiny perfect form,
kiss your forehead,
kiss your cheek
—yet I am afraid
of waking you.

JAMES GRADY

*The Hankering Lion*

the hankering green lion of spring roves
and through a vent in her velvet jeans
one black lace flower on her mesh panties
peeks. we two dream, strewn in the blue heat.
what she wants well who knows but now she smiles,
her eyes shut, as her hand brushes my wrist.
so I tuck my Seth Thomas wristwatch
under that plump flower.
she leaves it there. now on the oozing hill
oh I hear the flowers grow and the watch
use its little gold hands.

SALLY STERN

*Wait, I've Been This Way Before*

Wait
I've been this way before.
I know these shapes
And textures under blind fingers.

I know that I shall be the sea
And the mother
And never me.
Wait
I am here
Under the sea
Recognize me.

Tongue tempted, teased
You reach, breathing
To break like sky-fires
In an inward breath
And then you kiss my mouth,
Then.
And rest
Like a child suckling
In its innocence.

All right it's not me
It's the mother and the sea.

WILLIAM MORRIS

*poem for a girl i booted*

shall i say that to me
you were as lasting as a cloud
you who are so catlike
with your eyes of agate
with your breasts of fruit
webbed with your hair of silk

shall i tell of your kiss
the fever of your lips
the invitation to destroy myself
to be devoured without regrets
in the flame of your thighs

you are the sea
in all its moods & colors
the times of tranquillity
the fury of your sudden storms
who lured me as greeks were lured
who fondled me with soft waves
then threw me against the rocks

what shall i say of you
i who have the sunrage in my eyes
the moons madness in my mind
the manspike for your frame of flowers

what shall i say
having promised you a poem
even so
what could be more a poem
than the sight of you
high over the city & harbor
with the wind fingering your hair
indeed what could be

Ted Joans

Playmates

"*Whenever I meet some old buddies from Indiana University its the same old questions they ask—why aren't you painting, what's all this clowning publicity for, since when are you a poet? Well, I'm not really a poet except for Allen Ginsberg who grabbed· me one November day in nineteen fifty eight and said he was bored stiff with reading in the coffee shop and why didn't I do it because I was great. He insisted I go with him and try. I tell you I was scared silly at first but it all worked out and now I'm making more money than I ever made from my painting. At least now I have enough coming in steady to keep the family on Staten Island well off.  And I still paint too you know in my studio at Astor Place. As for all the showoff stunts well hell that's just part of the job and making a living.*"

Let's play something. Let's play anything. Let's drive around town and
sling paint at happylooking people
and throw shovels into store front
church windows.

Let's play something. Let's play something daring. Let's all go to Central
Park at midnight and strip . . . then
piss on everyone we encounter.

Let's play something. Let's play something sexy . . . like getting into bed
dressed complete . . . even adding
overcoat and gloves . . . and then try
to copulate through all that clothing
and give a prize to the first one that
has a climax without physical contact.

Let's play something. Let's play something horrible. You be Hitler and you
be Mussolini and you be Stalin and
you be Tojo, and you be Strijdom of
South Africa and I'll be Gov. Faubus.
Wow! What a cast of devils! Yeah,
let's play that.

Let's play something. Let's play anything. Let's play bohemian, and wear
odd clothes, and grow a beard or a
ponytail, live in the Village for 200.00
a month for one small pad and stroll
through Washington Square Park with
a guitar and a chick looking sad.

Let's play something. Let's play that we
are all adult westerns, and we have
four big lying sponsors on TV . . . and
let's not use our guns or horses, but
use psychology and ride women at
night on the indoor prairie.

Let's play something. Let's play that we
are all Ivy Leaguers with belts in the
back of all articles of clothing includ-
ing our socks and ties.

Let's play that we are all creeps. Let's
play that we hang out with the 42nd St.
perverts and sit in the smelly movies
all daylong and urinate under the
seats.

Let's play that we are all SAFE. Let's
play that we all work from 9 to 5 and
we are trying to pay for that split
level home in Westchester and the
wall to wall carpets and the never
ending payments on the flashy car,
color TV, hi-fi, wash'n dry, deep
freeze and the other-keeping-up-with-
the-Jones deals.

Let's play something. Let's play anything. Let's play that we are all po-
licemen and be called the fuzz. Let's
play that we are all politicians and be
called crooked. Let's play that we are
all balletdancers and be called queers.
Let's play that we are all poets, and
be called beatniks. Let's play that we
are all artists and be called crazy.
Let's play that we are all Square Con-
ventional Spoiled American females.

Let's play something. Let's play anything. Let's play that we are all hip-
sters . . . and be spiritually involved
with life and dig all things creative
. . . and ball a whole lot . . . and be
happy in poetry and art . . . and travel
all over the world, digging everything
loving every swinging soul, picking up
on all jazz, experiencing all great kicks,
be chicks & cats avoiding conformity,
confessing the truth, disaffiliated with
goof, digging freedom, and wail cool
before the world.

Ted Joans' biannual birthday party at his Astor Place studio

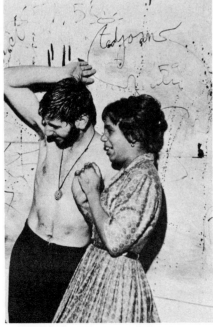

Hugh Romney

David Galler
Paul Goodman
Richard Higgins
Howard Hart
Marc D. Schleifer
Hugh Romney

*In this kingdom of illusions we grope for stays and foundations. There is none but a strict and faithful dealing at home and a severe barring out of all duplicity or illusion there. Whatever games are played with us, we must play no games with ourselves, but deal in our privacy with the last honesty and truth.*
*Ralph Waldo Emerson*

DAVID GALLER

*The Apology*

They who themselves had not a thread
To give gave me the maze instead—
Well-lit, at every alley's end
A couch from which I could pretend
For spells, dozing before the fine
Prints in their gold, sipping the wine
From fey decanters, that what was here
Was all, sufficing to rout desire
To explore. Yet as I paced,
Content for then, I was encased
By walls, one of which fell (a wall
Only by willed belief that all
Those alleys' ends were not the same)
That showed the way by which I came.
Strung by old smells into the gloom,
I was in turn led by the room
I had just left to think each crypt
Unique; the way the water dripped
From the cold stone my fingers found
Distinct urged that I claim this ground.
Yet, as I knelt in happiness,
Always my fingers would transgress
Across a tatter of silk, a gem,
Or antiquated eyeglass rim,
Beneath them touch upon a bone;
And I recalled who'd wept alone
In all those handsome alleys' ends
For years and had made no amends,
It seemed, but me to tunnels strewn
Between. Not the importune
And endless transferring of poor
Remains from chilled bewildering floor

To lighted niche and back is my
Apology, but that a wry
Laughter has left my lips each time
The wine is sipped or knees begrime
The dark, who know that I fulfill
These bones, wishing them clothed to kill.

PAUL GOODMAN

*Little Prayers* (*selections*)

My world, my only! as I see
soberly the necessity
    that thus I fail, and my hurts
    proportioned to my just deserts;

that's fine! as any truth is fine.
But that I change I do not find
    nor that I triumph by embrac-
    ing my fate, nor that I suffer less.

       ❀    ❀    ❀

Creator spirit, who dost lightly hover
whence I know not, and why to me I never
    questioned, come. Do visit thy lover
    after thy long absence. I turn over

awaking in the morning, thou art not
there to my touch, nor is a substitute
    there, but nothing, nothing at all to talk
    to and make love when I awake.

       ❀    ❀    ❀

By trials too hard for me beset
with awkward courage toward my death
    I stagger, every usual
    task I perform and, as I fail,

fashion the art-works to me given.
But lust is mercifully riven
    from me with hope, for always our
    task is measured to our power.

DICK HIGGINS

*The Pendulum*

Dangling dangling
I dunno but it seems to me as how
Dangling dangling
There isn't no way out so move along
Dangling dangling
The motion was in the cards
It was forced on you
Dangling dangling
The card you've drawn is the hanged man
Roughly observation without participation
Dangling Dangling
Just do something
Don't matter if it's the wrong thing
Dangling dangling
You've drawn the hanged man

HOWARD HART

*Angel*

Angel
Who was walked with me
 down nine hundred alleys
And who has re-adhered me
 to the floating wounds of Christ
Re-adhered me to blood and water
 to busted skin and the pain
 that is in open flesh
That has spared me most of the pain
Knowing a baby is easily shocked

Angel
You sleep on my eyelids
And the sand you leave for the morning
Is for some seashore far away
Some sea with a name I can't pronounce

Angel named Max
Because I'm sure that's your name
When we began to be friends
I looked straight into your eyes
And saw a lot of fire
You scare me
                Angel

Rain drops are not more simple
That clutter our eyes

MARC D. SCHLEIFER

*To Fidel Castro Somewhere in the Sierra Maestre*

In 1936 my father read the sunday papers—
I was one year old, not one and twenty
bleeding on some dusty road to Barcelona, weeping by the river
      Ebro—
Now, two decades later
Fidel, your picture is cod cake wrapping for my kitchen table.
Companero, we are closer than the A.P.
or bookshelf Atlas would have it
Not that I am there when you blow a bridge, build a barricade
put fear in the hearts of Cuban cops—
Courage is too concrete for the poet to claim abstractly;
But you, amigo, are with me
at the Supermarket, planning the destruction of the A. & P.
With me when I light the mystic match of protest—
Senor you are my keeper.


I have no quarrel
with the old man who does not hope to turn again
I dig the furies, the draughty and decaying house—
the stain that is forever, and
cannot be recalled by a ballot box.
But the great books lie
man lives, the Spirit is what withers—
Fidel Castro, you may win a razor and turn clean-cut
grow a collar, become tomorrow's tax collector
Still, this moment's man is this moment's Spirit
Spirit that rocked Berlin tanks with brick and stone
marched to Czar Palace on Easter Sunday
shouted Viva el Cristo Rey at Red Shirt riflemen
died for verse and a lady's honor in lonely Utah—
Does the Cadi with a union label diminish a wobbly's song
and should I forsake Potemkin if the Commissar takes his martini
      dry?
cracked walls, inevitable sagging structure predicted
before a solitary brick is even put in place
Yea the Spirit warps in a contractor's hand, only the demolition
      squads know God.
From the smoke of burnt museum and charred Cathedral
Angels descend among us.

HUGH ROMNEY

*joes song*

once upon
and eversince
i was a child
in a childs world

i have wept a childs tears
and built a childs wall
of clay and stone
and colored years
of poems in paint
and virgins gold

i sought to build
a wall so tall
of lion eggs
from galilee
a brick of song
among the dregs
of silver nails
and lesser men
—a mile long
to kiss the sun
and climb again

once ago
and ever now
i stood a man
on a childs wall

i stopped and prayed
to spiderwebs
and roses of the sea
i spoke as one
with all the earth
and knew the pain
of birth and death
to be the same
without my wall

once upon
and everfurled
i stand alone
with all the world

Lawrence Ferlinghetti

Tentative Description of a Dinner Given to Promote the
Impeachment of President Eisenhower

*When Larry was in for a short visit, I suggested he come over
the house for a Sunday dinner with the family especially since
his wife hadn't arrived yet and he seemed kind of lonely. My
wife's stew was great, the wine good, and the children behaved
themselves for a change. Afterwards we took a walk and I
showed him the Heights—Brooklyn Bridge, where Hart Crane
lived, the Promenade, the view of downtown Manhattan and
the Bay, Truman Capote's house and Louis Zukofsky's. Finally
we walked on Cranberry Street to the Walt Whitman plaque
commemorating the spot where the first edition of* Leaves of
Grass *was printed. On the way back home, Larry kept remark-
ing on the necessity for a poet to perceive the littlest details
of the world around him, to see everything, to register everything, to think about everything.*

With Allen Ginsberg and Don Allen, editor and translator

Photograph facing page 131: A Reading at The Living Theatre

After it became obvious that the strange rain would never stop
And after it became obvious that the President was doing everything
    in his power
And after it became obvious that the President's general staff
    was still in contact with the President deep in the heart
    of Georgia while deep in the heart of South America the
    President's left-hand man was proving all the world loves
    an American
And after it became obvious that the strange rain would never stop
    and that Old Soldiers never drown and that roses in the rain
    had forgotten the word for bloom and that perverted pollen
    blown on sunless seas was eaten by irradiated fish who spawned up
    cloudleaf streams and fell onto our dinnerplates
And after it became obvious that the President was doing every thing
    in his power to make the world safe for nationalism
    his brilliant military mind never having realized
    that nationalism itself was the idiotic superstition
    which would blow up the world
And after it became obvious that the President nevertheless still
    carried no matter where he went in the strange rain the little
    telegraph key which like a can opener could be used instantly
    to open but not to close the hot box of final war if not to
    waylay any stray assinine action by any stray assinine second
    lieutenant pressing any strange button anywhere far away over an
    arctic ocean thus illuminating the world once and for all

With Robert MacGregor of New Directions and Theatre Arts

And after it became obvious that the law of gravity was still
     in effect and that what blows up must come down on everyone
     including white citizens
And after it became obvious that the Voice of America was really
     the Deaf Ear of America and that the President was unable
     to hear the underprivileged natives of the world shouting
     No Contamination Without Representation in the strange rain
     from which there was no escape- except Peace
And after it became obvious that the word Truth had only a comic
     significance to the Atomic Energy Commission while the
     President danced madly to mad Admiral Straus waltzes
     wearing
     special atomic earplugs which prevented him from hearing
     Albert Schweitzer and nine thousand two hundred and thirty five
     other scientists telling him about spastic generations and
     blind boneless babies in the rain from which there was no
     escape- except Peace
And after it became obvious that the President was doing every
     thing
     in his power to get thru the next four years without eating
     any of the crates of irradiated vegetables wellwishers had
     sent him from all over and which were filling the corridors
     and antechambers and bedchambers and chamberpots in the
     not-so-White House not to mention all the other various
     Golf Houses scattered thruout the land of prosperity

And after it became obvious that the Great Soldier had become
        the Great Conciliator who had become the Great Compromiser
        who had become the Great Fence Sitter who actually had heard
        of the Supreme Court's decision to desegregate the land of
        the free and had not only heard of it but had actually
                                                        read it
And after it became obvious that the President had gone to
        Gettysburg fourscore and seven years ago and had given
        his Gettysburg Address to the postman and so dedicated
        himself to the unfinished task
                                Then it was that the natives
of the Republic began assembling in the driving rain from which
there was no escape- except Peace
                                And then it was that no
invitations had to be sent out for the great testimonial dinner
except to politicians whose respected names would lend weight
to the project but who did not come anyway suspecting the whole
thing was a plot to save the world from the clean bomb from
which there was no escape- except Peace
                                And women who still needed
despair to look truly tragic came looking very beautiful and
very tragic indeed since there was despair to spare
                                And some men also despaired
and sat down in Bohemia and were too busy to come

But other men came whose only
political action during the past twenty years had been to flush
a protesting toilet and run
And babies came in their
carriages carrying irradiated dolls and holding onto crazy strings
of illuminated weather baloons filled with Nagasaki air
And those who had not left
their TV sets long enough to notice the weather in seven years
now came swimming thru the rain holding their testimonials
And those came who had never marched
in sports car protest parades and those came who had never been
arrested for sailing a protesting Golden Rule in unpacific oceans
And Noah came in his own Ark looking
surprisingly like an outraged Jesus Christ and cruised about
flying his pinion and picking up two of each beast that wanted
to be preserved in the rain which was raining real cats and
dogs and from which there was no escape- except Peace
And peddlers came in lead jockstraps
selling hotdogs and rubber American flags and waving petitions
proclaiming it Unamerican to play golf on the same holy days
that clean bombs were set off on time
And finally after everyone who
was anyone and after everyone who was no one had arrived and after
every soul was seated and waiting for the symbolic mushroom soup
to be served and for the keynote speeches to begin
The President himself came in
Took one look around and said
We Resign

Allen Ginsberg introducing Michael McClure and Philip Whalen
to a City College literature class

Michael McClure
Philip Whalen
E. A. Navaretta
Barbara Ellen
Martin Last
Robert Hanlon

*Would the world be more beautiful were all our faces alike?*
*Were our tempers, our talents, our tastes, our forms, our*
*wishes, aversions and pursuits cast exactly in the same mold?*
*If no varieties existed in the animal, vegetable or mineral*
*creation, but all moved strictly uniform, catholic and orthodox,*
*what a world of physical and moral monotony would it be! These*
*are the absurdities into which those run who usurp the throne*
*of God and dictate to Him what He should have done.*
*Thomas Jefferson*

The City College class at the reading

MICHAEL McCLURE

## YES AND HANDS AND ARMS YES TABLE DARK SQUATTY AND STRONG

at night I lay in pain and sorrow,
in shadow I am a seraphim—miserable and sick

my dreams are not memories,
so much is blotted out that I am only here.
So much to remember, so much to remember, so much to remember.
This is a war. The instants
history.
(In the night I awoke and remembered you and you were gone
though you lay by my side. I searched for you among the silver
hangings, I could not speak your name. I wandered in the long hall.)
etc.

PHILIP WHALEN

*Sauced*

I go reeling down the hall
                    into the leaves!
Tree of heaven balcony door is open


            A trio for Jaybird, Telephone & Trambone
            Jay
            Jay
            Trambone: poo-poo-poo        POO!
            Jay
            Telephone
            Poo jay telebone
            Tram Sunday poo


The landlady explains the vacant room across the hall:
                    "Very quiet."


        Gold squirrel!
                        in pear tree
Surgeons the stem &                    (Campanile 5 PM)
                    pear wobbling in his no-chin-space
Leaps into heaven tree
The neighbors' pears
Jay            Jay
        (          )
        F-Train horn
Wren
            airplanes in the eaves like hornets

E. A. NAVARETTA

*On the Thin Air*

For Milton Resnick
the painter who has written

*The artist lives on thin air. What does he want to do;*
*does he think about—a grand march through new territory—a*
*wild gallop on dark land—a battle with ferocious hordes—a*
*beautiful somersault above hushed populace. Can he do any of*
*these eternaly worth-while things while being led softly by*
*hand and told to watch his step.*

*He must go where with every step his strength and interest*
*grow and grow.*

For I burn to consume
this light    this matter and so
        this atmosphere
              so thinly provided
        if I move I die
for the love
        and hunger sweetly
              only yes it can be
somebody deeply
        forever now


but I burn to consume
for all days
        known as the new
in taste of something
    and presently
        and here
              and also never
yes    really me
in space    so smash
    the light
        an eye on green


if the time
darkly always
    so swiftly
        so let it alone
    moving    stirring
    roughly tender
if tomorrow    if yesterday
        so bitterly
    today it exists
again growing
        before as blue

only I burn
        clothed consuming
    and renewed    this matter in
              becoming is real
underfoot nothing is
        but the eye
              rearing
              sensing
                    mindful totally
        flowing sharply
              in this time
              and named again
alone    myself
    and fitfully


for I insist    consuming
        for instance
    of thinnest space
            clawed yellow
                and eaten too
    so better this way
                to come anew
and if    mine to herald
                not to defend
    to believe for another
    unremembered is
completely here
    now    for a minute
                tensely and fair
        for nothing is
            so shafted    so
            trumpeted
                and sheer
from the eye
    my other
    O yes my other.

BARBARA  ELLEN

*Boris  Oblesow*

a torn sun where she lets go
the naive audacity
                    of her mouth.

in his mouth
                her dust of black seeds
thin murmur of the silkbird's killed wound.

void
        the mind clears where shame.
the day-wasp cries once raucous
                            3-eyed
black pearl

the mind's star unhinged
disrobes
            a brown bear eyeing honey
where a tinkle of birds
mumble
            in the blue hair
of the mountain.

MARTIN LAST

*Anton Bruckner: Musician*

From the ears
      straight lines to the
         spine
granted      the heart knows
here are all yeses

Yes    he knew it all
    clear soul    clean bowel
blood blooming in great space
      to glory
Tarry in the macrocosm, Anton—
         walking on the ground
Hail Prevails
    this is wholly Hallelujah!

ROBERT  HANLON


87.

if castration rewarded
greatness

                SUCH AN HONOR

to hear

      "They're off!"


88.

ALL  DEMOSTHENES  IS  DIVIDED!

- - - - - - - - - - - - - - -

cassandra prob
ably

      started wars
    all through

        his

tory

   by shrilling against
  them

and pebbles be

     FORE!

        Phillipics

  be

     COME?

       Gaul

         stones

of victory

    dem
    ago

     gues gargoyle with

         BLOOD

Clint Nichols

John Brent

William Millet

William Berkson

A. B. Spellman

Ed Freeman

Barbara Guest

William V. Ward

A sheaf of young writers in Greewich Village

Ambrose Hollingsworth

Bob Lubin

Jimmy Lyons

Steve Levine

Tony Jordan

Margaret Randall

George Stade

Daisy Alden

William Godden

Michael Rapach

Joel Oppenheimer

Tad Sadowsky

Kirby Doyle

Edward Marshall

Albert Saijo, Lew Welch and Jack Kerouac

This is what it's called

*Albert, Lew and Jack had just arrived from Frisco and Fred had arranged for Lew to come to his apartment to take some photographs. When Lew came, he said that Albert and Jack were downstairs and was it all right if they came up too. Fred said of course and Gloria got some beer from the refrigerator. When they decided to write the poem together, Fred put on the lights which were very bright and uncomfortable. He kept snapping while they composed and Gloria typed it all down. Finally they finished but when it came to reading it aloud, Jack said it was about time they turned off the bright lights and that was the end of the picture taking.*

*This is what it's called—*

## THIS IS A POEM BY ALBERT SAIJO, LEW WELCH AND JACK KEROUAC

At the second coming I want my navy knit cap
(Worn inside out).
I insist on my survival diaphragm; what am I, a girl?
No more immaculate conceptions.
Oh, let's get really poetic.
Big white space

The lorn are rude to the turning shoe
Which is literally true, they have one in Lost Davis
Angel ma

In Lost Davis there is a motel called the Blue Angel with an 18
foot blue angel with big tits spinning in the winter desert air.
Hippopotamuses are gigantic river pigs
Grain elevators are giant trucks waiting for the road to approach them
East St. Louis: whore candy

I'd like to sleep in Joplin in little snatches
It began to snow lightly in southern Illinois
There were rabbit tracks in motel driveways
The interminable potato cooker gossiped
JK: "What's the local Indian saying around here?"
Indian: "There are none around here."
> *I pledge to my customers as a Texaco dealer*
> *that my registered bathroom shall remain*
> *fully equipped and clean.*
Isn't that sick?

Thou irk'st but for gain
Gloria you aren't getting the punctuation

I saw a white horse standing
In an abandoned store front

I knew the misery of the east
I heard that dog barking behind the mangy door
He was guarding the door nobody wanted

The last time I was in Amarillo
I smoked my first cigar
And Roosevelt died.

In log cabin motel
New Lincolns
Dream Van Doren.

I turned into a gas station
The engine stopped.

In Safeway parking lots
Old men drive slowly
Backwards.

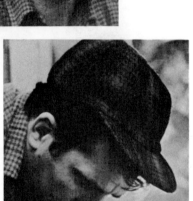

In Arizona they put a cross beside the highway wherever somebody is killed. Large cross for adults, small cross for children.
Seeing these we said let's stop and steal one. It was sunset. Purple
cowboys with mouths of dust were ranging far for the heifer of
the Lord. Ran out of the car, saw the tip of the cross against the
Arizona sunset, and said I have to see it. Knelt. Forced to kneel.
Found myself kneeling in thorns.

In Texas
Leo's cock
Turned to glass.
And he wrapped it in gold foil.

Driving across the U.S.A. 75 miles an hour
Leo with his cock of port
Passing trains

When milady dreams
I dream of thinking

When milady unbuckles her pursey eye
I count her shoe tongues.
And dream of 14 year old Puerto Rican girls
with Balthus eyes.

                    Villon yslipped tresors into his boys.


On a disappearing road
Among crenelated mountains
Thinking about whores:
          *That girl in Chicago in a tub of oysters.*

Left the civilized plains of the middle west
for the mountain canyons, flora fauna of New York

Everyone goes home alone
Under the 2,000 foot ceiling of Manhattan

"Spring evening—
The sound of the frog
Jumping in the pond"—Basho

"Midday sun—
The mad girl singing
In the boat"—Basho

Whiter than the rocks of white mountain
This autumn wind—Basho

Shiro yama no
Ishi yori shiroshi
Aki no kase—Basho
Hail to Harold Goldfinger

Ray Bremser reading at the Artist's Studio

Gregory Corso
Peter Orlovsky
Philip Lamantia
Jack Micheline
Joseph LeSueur
Ray Bremser

*The melancholy prudence of the abandonment of such a great being as a man is, to the toss and pallor of years of money-making, with all their scorching days and icy nights, and all their stifling deceits and underhand dodgings, or infinitesimals of parlors, or shameless stuffing while others starve, and all the loss of the bloom and odor of the earth, and of the flowers and atmosphere, and of the sea, and of the true taste of the women and the men you pass or have to do with in youth or middle age, and the issuing sickness and desperate revolt at the close of a life without elevation or naivete (even if you have achieved a secure 10,000 a year, or election to Congress or the Governorship) and the ghastly chatter of a death without serenity or majesty, is the great fraud upon modern civilization and forethought, blotching the surface and system which civilization undeniably drafts, and moistening with tears the immense features it spreads and spreads with such velocity before the reach'd kisses of the soul.*

*Walt Whitman*

GREGORY CORSO

*Sura*

Pinch the air that its shriek might break silence
Nature is done.
The seasons have ended their alliance
And so the sun.

Twist the elf's knotty arm it must drawl thuds of pain:
Light must return
And reprieve the earth with its merciful stain.
—Fairy, tip the urn.

Think like a clock with no time to tell.
Hear the knell of your thoughts and wonder the bell.
Leave your sights of life nor comprehend fear
—Death is not anywhere near.

Hurry! Mountains are falling on valleys.
Trees are getting lost.
—Is this the one? Is that the one? Which tree was it?
I remember distinctly there was a difference among them.
Can I see one tree, know it well, and knowing, see all trees?—
Quick! Quick! Oceans are slipping into other oceans.
Fear not! Nothing can break your heart.
Life has it you make the Crack
And like the nail that meets the hammer
Depart.
Not the fly with your magnitude wonder why.
Yourself wonder but with silence and sly.
Watch you move from pot to pan—don't cry.
No thing can ever break your heart.
When your dreams are fullest the cruel hammer will blow
And die at your heart.
Too late! The sky is brown.

PETER ORLOVSKY

*Lines of Feelings*

The mountain bear has a hole in his pants—trouble.
Doctors get free passes to my museum
in return for their lobotomies on me.
I am not afraid to work—I would love to fly a dirigible.
Nor am I afraid to be a collector of lamps—
provided everyone helps me.
And as for your cantelopes, 2 for 29—I consider it dangerous.
My fortune is dedicated to going to see movies.
I don't go anywhere without my belt,
cause I own everything that lays inside my belt.
And when ever there's a man on the corner
telling me there's a boat leaving for heaven now,
I'll go & never speak another word.

There was this fellow I was telling you about
who built something in his room, he built & built
until it got too big for his room, then he had to move,
then he always had to move, that was him.
Then this new fellow who went out to the store
and he walked & he walked, and one block went behind him,
then another, then another ahead & that went behind him,
& so on till he was far away from home—
all because of the way somebody said something on T.V.

O science give me twenty feet
twenty Grandma meat ball eyes
take me apart in the robot room
just give me one thing extraordinary
    (I got something going here now,
      don't rush me, I got this typewriter, right
      got this paper here, right
      all alone, right—)

Walking over to put music on phonograph space,
bringing cover (of composer) back to desk to see how it's spelt—
Pictures at Exhibition by Musorsky

but this room is all alone
with too much of myself in it.

But yet, how much beauty has rolled off the breast of a dying swan
that lay cooling on the grass while the Host is shaving its shadow?

PHILIP LAMANTIA

*Fud at Foster's*

Bowl of cold turkie fool
A roast chicken liver louie
My cigarillo's going out in a spanish bedroom
Jazz is for free
Coke is for free
Junk's unlimited and sold by Agents
      that I can make poems that I spin the day to
      Tim Buck Two that I lose tension and head
      floats forever a far inscape of lemon trees AND
NO MORE REALITY SANDWICHES! ! !

Can I ever get up from this table?
Can I ever stop thunder?
Can I make it to windows of fur?
Can I soup up her eyes in a can of star milk and shoot it for
                                    light?

Can I read in the park?
Can I sit on the Moon? Can I?
Oh, stop it! Oh start! Oh, make music
Though your arm is too thin
   and the jails are too small, sweaty AND STINK!

## JACK MICHELINE

I tell you
I tell you
All people are enslaved
I tell you
I tell you
All people are enslaved
in these modern times
the people are so nervous
the people don't believe
the people feel so insecure
All people are enslaved
All people are enslaved
I tell you
I tell you
in these modern times
the people are so nervous
the people are so ill at ease
in these modern times
people don't believe
people don't believe
All people
All people
All people are enslaved
I tell you
I tell you
All people are enslaved

JOSEPH LeSUEUR

*The Castle*

Always before it has been of a sordid nature.
I did not face my adversaries bravely.
I neither fought for my life nor accepted death.
For example, I allowed those two Japanese robbers
to chase me down winding, darkened streets,
firing at me, at last finding their mark.
Another time a large Negro appeared
from behind a garbage can. He knifed me.
Once it was a sinking ship.
I went down without a struggle,
I did not try to swim.
And on each occasion in the past
consciousness would come just before death:
I would stir myself awake,
as though life were an escape.

This time it is different.
There is a castle surrounded by a wall.
No harm will fall me as long as I stay
within the shadow of the wall,
away from the castle.
What happens is inevitable:
the wall cracks, tired from its own weight.
I flee, not away from the castle
but to it, into it. I climb stairs.
I stand alone in my castle
and look out on the valleys of my life,
which stretch as far as the eye can reach,
green here, barren there.
And I am neither sad nor happy.
It is curiously what I expected.
The castle gates were always open, waiting.

Next time I hope to run the other way
into those valleys, the barren parts:
the refuge of my castle does not interest me.

RAY BREMSER

*Song to a Silo*

huge tit-topped slatted stack
tile-like your weird walls stinking.
straight profundis-candle without light
and only corn to call your guttage—

climbed your innards on the swollen stair
strewn with whiffs of dairy.

shoveled half your cancer down an odd
posterior canal.

hoisted tons of self gone heaven bound—
but only knew you as a drunken vial
where never-tasted nectar sunk its weight
in blue-sward vivid aromatic depth.

mighty silo!
worked my arms to early death
cried my eyes with fire
and my nose imbibed.

walked your silly circle
for the grace of cow's milk
chest and twenty pounds.

fell away from farmers-lung
and terrible diseases of the head
gone blind with hooch,
I laid me down ten feet away
to finally end my torment toil
and dream your corn-bred nightmare
all about two talking silos,
saying

"he's a bug within us,
not our own!"
                    "let's conspire
murder then, and one day
when a cow shits out its curds
his face and age and wrinkles will caress
the funny gutter, and remember
how his visions had had other silage days!"

Jon Adams

Robert Cordier

Dick Dabney

Taylor Mead

May Swenson reading at the Nicholas Cafe

Jud Yalkut          Steve Tropp reading at the Gaslight Cafe

Thomas McGrath

Kenneth Patchen reading with the Charles Mingus Band

Larry Rivers                           Jean Garrigue

Willard Maas                              Edward Field